Y0-ATD-050

The Vineyard & The Sea

Poems by
Charles Wharton Stork
1881-1971

With a foreword by
Henry Beetle Hough

1977

The Athenaeum of Philadelphia

© The Athenæum of Philadelphia,
1977
ISBN: 0-916530-07-8

Contents

FOREWORD

Martha's Vineyard had a special meaning for Charles Wharton Stork, and this volume of his poems reveals it still, as if the appointment he kept during so many Island days and weeks were a tryst to which any sharer of his feeling could return today. The poems are his response to the companionship of sea, shore, dunes, fog, clouds, and times of year.

His was a generous response, and those who knew him in the seasons these poems represent find themselves knowing him again in the relationship a poet of nature always seeks to establish. He gave of himself in a simplicity of line and imagery that ring true to his purpose now as then.

The poems are best read in the reflection of his personality and as a memorial to a spirit that sought and found fulfillment on its own terms.

HENRY BEETLE HOUGH

Edgartown,
October 1, 1975

Gathering of poets and literary figures of the 1920's. Standing in the rear (left to right): John Hall Wheelock, Elinor Wylie, William Rose Benét, and David Morton; front row: Leonora Speyer, Marguerita Wilkinson, Howard Trowbridge Pulsifer, Charles Wharton Stork, and Maxwell Bodenheim. This cartoon appeared in the *New York Times* on May 13, 1923.

CHARLES WHARTON STORK

(1881–1971)

The author of "The Vineyard and the Sea" was descended from a German family which emigrated to America in 1788 and produced several outstanding Lutheran ministers. His father, Theophilus Baker Stork, whom the poet described as "an intellectual, a born philosopher and jurist," followed the law for a short period, wrote books on ethical and religious subjects, and shrewdly managed the family money that came his way. He lived in Philadelphia and married Hannah Wharton of the outstanding industrial family that built up a 99,000-acre estate (now a state forest) around Batsto, New Jersey. The family is also known for founding the Wharton School of Finance and Commerce of the University of Pennsylvania.

The poet was born to this couple on February 12, 1881. When he was five, his mother died and was succeeded five years later by a second Quaker mother, Anna Brown Cope, who struggled to make the independent boy conform to her narrow notions of what was proper. Without siblings, the boy readily absorbed the scholarly atmosphere of the elegant home, read widely from the large library, and learned to enjoy a world created by his active imagination. He attended a private Quaker day school, Germantown Friends, and graduated in 1898.

Until he was in college, Wharton, as he was called, spent his summers at "Bræcleugh," his grandfather Wharton's large summer home near Jamestown, Rhode Island, which was a ferry ride away from Newport, a fashionable summer resort and a major Navy base. He wrote glowingly of the warm, harmonious Quaker household, which included many servants and a boat captain, and the cultured atmosphere that featured chess, whist, and a variety of family music, including piano solos and duets that he performed. He appreciated the spectacular view from "Bræcleugh," perched on a cliff 150 feet above Narragansett Bay, swam daily, fished, played along the ever-intriguing beaches and rocks, and in long hours by himself developed his great love of nature, sharpened his observation, and indulged his penchant for daydreaming. The effects of this idyllic life, with its isolation from the nitty gritty and the problems of the workaday world, can be observed in his writings and in his entire career. He also began his tennis career, which lasted into his seventies and reached a late climax in 1920 with the winning of the Northeast Harbor men's doubles tournament.

In the fall of 1898 Wharton enrolled in Haverford College, located in Philadelphia's "Main Line" area and known for its serious Quaker outlook and its high scholastic standing. Here he played on cricket and chess teams, kept up his music, and deepened his already considerable scholarship. Majoring in English and Greek, he graduated Phi Beta Kappa in 1902.

After making the first of many trips to Europe in the summer of 1902, Mr. Stork attended Harvard, where he specialized in English, particularly the Elizabethan drama, and earned his M.A. in 1903. He played varsity cricket, was active in college literary circles, and had poems published in the *Harvard Advocate*.

In the fall of 1903 he began studying for his doctorate and teaching in the English Department of the University Pennsylvania. After receiving his Ph.D. in 1905, he continued to teach but took European trips, as indicated in the Chronology section of this volume, to widen his growing knowledge and develop his exceptional aptitude for languages. During his studies of the German language and literature in Munich in 1907–1908, he met and married Elisabeth von Pausinger of Salzburg, the youngest of the four daughters of the distinguished artist Franz von Pausinger, who did commissions for Crown Prince Rudolph and other Austrian notables.

The young bride, who was a painter and musician, came to Philadelphia in 1908 and soon presided over "Birdwood," Dr. Stork's 16-acre estate in North Philadelphia. Here he used his inherited wealth to support a staff of servants and an elaborate establishment that left him free to teach, carry on his literary work, entertain poets and other creative people, and keep up with the cultural world that he loved.

From 1908 to 1916 Dr. Stork continued to teach at the University of Pennsylvania and to write poetry, some of which appeared in periodicals. By the latter date he had published three slim volumes of poetry in the classic mold and *Sea and Bay,* a book-length narrative poem that grew out of the summers in Rhode Island. He had also written scholarly articles and contributed translations of a play and many poems to a set of books called *The German Classics.* Meanwhile the birth of a daughter and two sons had aroused such interest in the Pausingers that they persuaded the Storks to come to Salzburg in the summer of 1914 with the little ones. About the time of the happy reunion, however, the European war clouds began to gather, and during the frantic rush of tourists back to America the little family was fortunate to secure passage and get home safely.

In 1916 Dr. Stork, who had attained the position of Assistant Professor, resigned from the University of Pennsylvania. In this year he published the *Selected Poems of Gustaf Fröding,* his first Scandinavian translation, which marked his entry into a new field in which he was to be very active and successful. It is interesting to note parenthetically that in the years following the war Mrs. Stork was also busy as a translator, rendering about eight German children's books, including *Heidi,* into English. Another new venture, begun in 1917, was the editing of *Contemporary Verse,* a monthly magazine. Although the project, like most others of its kind, lost money, Dr. Stork continued until 1926 in order to give young and unknown writers a chance to be heard. His files for this period are full of letters of thanks from aspiring poets who broke into print in *Contemporary Verse* and who received valuable personal criticism and encouragement from the editor.

The decade from the end of World War I to the stock market crash of 1929 was one of great literary activity, of achievement and recognition for Dr. Stork. He saw the publication of ten volumes that he edited or translated. He studied the drama seriously and made numerous trips to New York to keep abreast of developments on Broadway. In 1925 his dramatic fantasy *The Flower Seller* won a national prize offered by the Plays and Players theater group, which performed the play the following year. In 1929 his historical play *Ninon,* which dealt with Ninon de Lenclos and other luminaries of the time of Louis XIV, was produced across the Hudson from New York in Hackensack. Pursuing his great interest in Swedish literature, Dr. Stork made trips to Sweden in 1920 and 1923 and had his verse translations published in various periodicals and poetry collections. Critic Holger Lundbergh, reviewing some of these translated poems in *The American-Scandinavian Review,* wrote that "the Stork renditions seem well-nigh perfect" and preserve "in some magic fashion the poet's spirit and dreams and heart-beats." The Swedish government considered this work so significant that King Gustavus V personally decorated the translator with the order of Gustaf Vasa, First Class, for his services in making Swedish literature known to the English-speaking world. Other honors that Dr. Stork earned were his election to the presidency of the Poetry Society of America in 1926, his inclusion in *Who's Who in America,* and his selection (somewhat later) as one of the ten most distinguished alumni of Haverford College.

During this decade of peak activity and success, Dr. Stork also wrote critical essays, book reviews, and a little fiction; furthermore, he gave occasional lectures and poetry readings and toward the end began a brief period as editor of "The Archer," an international cultural magazine published by the Society of the Friends of Roerich (a Russian painter). With all these activities and membership in several cultural organizations, Dr. Stork met many literary people and was an accepted member of the top echelon of poets. In addition to the writers shown in the cartoon, he knew Robert Frost, Vachel Lindsay (both of whom were his house guests), Carl Sandburg, Edwin Arlington Robinson, Ezra Pound, Archibald Macleish, Louis Untermeyer, Amy Lowell, Eugene O'Neill, Gene Stratton Porter, John Masefield, Selma Lagerlöf (Swedish Nobel Prize winner), and many others.

The stock market crash of 1929, in which Dr. Stork lost heavily, marked a turning point in the nation's economic, social, and cultural life. The literary world, which had for some time been changing under the impact of postwar cynicism and new concepts of poetry, suffered not only the effects of depression and reduced markets but major changes of mood and style. The pace of life was accelerating, science was becoming a dominant force, the world was concerned with new interests, complex problems, and above all with survival. The mounting pressures of modern life, the information explosion, radio, sports, travel, and later television squeezed pleasure reading down to a minimum. Dr. Stork's classicism, his love of simple things in nature, his search for Beauty, Truth, and God, and his faith in traditional moral values seemed old-fashioned, irrelevant. Accordingly, few of the many poems he continued to write were published, editors were little interested in what he had to say as a critic and scholar, and his name quietly slipped into the background.

However, despite the rejection slips, Dr. Stork remained confident of the value of his creations and continued his varied literary work into the 1960s, when his physical and mental powers declined. The Bibliography indicates that he was prolific in translations from Swedish and branched out into Norwegian and Danish. 1933 saw the first and only publication of any of his novels, "Sunset Harbor: A Modern Idyll," which was based on the vacation life he saw in his many summers spent at Northeast Harbor, on Mt. Desert Island, Maine. Clinging to his hopes of a Broadway success, he wrote more plays and had an off-Broadway production of his "Quaker Mother" in 1936.

In 1935, after almost two decades, Dr. Stork returned to teaching, giving courses in literature and creative writing at Harcum Junior College in Bryn Mawr. In contrast to his experience on the Pennsylvania faculty, he enjoyed the work and was unhappy to have it end in 1951 as the result of bankruptcy.

Just before this, in 1948, appeared his first book of original poetry since 1916, "On Board Old Ironsides: A Rope-Yarn Epic," a 92-page story of the War of 1812 at sea. In 1948 he was at work on a companion volume dealing with the Navy's role in World War II in the Pacific. As part of the research he traveled as the guest of the Secretary of the Navy from Hawaii to China aboard the aircraft carrier *Princeton.* When "NAVPAC" was published in 1952, the late Vice Admiral Oscar C. Badger, the author's host in Tsingtau, commended the new epic as follows: "It is a fascinating story, wonderfully well conceived and presented, true to fact in its historical passages, and delightful to read."

At this point I take the liberty of adding a note of my own concerning Dr. Stork's sea poetry. He spent almost every summer on the seashore: at Jamestown, Northeast Harbor, and finally at Chilmark, Martha's Vineyard, where Mrs. Stork took the initiative to acquire property and build a cottage overlooking the Atlantic. From these vantage points he studied the ocean and its coastal waters for over three-quarters of a century. He and Mrs. Stork alone experienced the fury of a hurricane which cut off electricity, telephone, and access to the major portion of Martha's Vineyard and which threatened to do serious damage to the lightly built Chilmark cottage. These experiences plus many ocean voyages and the events recounted in "Sketches by an Athenian" gave him an exceptional feeling and background for writing about the sea. Accordingly, consideration of his three book-length narrative poems and the lyrics in the present volume might prompt the suggestion that Charles Wharton Stork has some claim to the title of "The American Masefield."

In between the two Navy poems he published "Hearts and Voices," a volume of poems dealing with the great composers of the world. As evidence that the poet was again in a very congenial field, it should be noted that he kept playing piano for pleasure as long as health permitted, that he composed short piano pieces and songs, that he improvised character sketches of his friends, attended innumerable concerts and operas, wrote two opera libretti, and knew many musicians, including Leopold Stokowski, to whom the "Prelude Before the Symphony," which opens the volume, is dedicated.

Two more titles complete the list of Dr. Stork's published works. *A Vision of Misjudgment,* a short fantasy satirizing T. S. Eliot and other nontraditional poets, was published in 1958. In 1967, long after it was written, *Alcibiades: A Play of Athens in the Great Age* was printed by Syracuse University. Until the end he maintained his hopes that this drama, which he called his most important, would be performed and bring him the popular success that he had sought long and earnestly.

Dr. Stork had a sound constitution, did calisthenics, swam, played tennis year after year, and adhered to a sensible physical routine; all this combined to make him unusually healthy through most of his life. Toward the 1960s, however, his strength gradually declined, and various ailments followed. He died peacefully on May 22, 1971, at the age of 90.

Charles Wharton Stork was six feet tall, well-proportioned, and had sandy hair and moustache and sky-blue eyes which could change rapidly from twinkling humor to stern severity. "I fell in love with life and have never recovered," he wrote in his unpublished autobiography. He was fortunate in being able to an exceptional degree to do what he wanted, and justified his good fortune with the zest he put into his varied activities. He carried through each of his innumerable writings or projects with confidence and enthusiasm, and if one work was rejected, he had no doubt that his current project, or the next, would be successful. He was equally absorbed in his recreation and other activities and would fight for every point in the most ordinary club tennis match or family bridge game. He was a keen baseball fan—he wrote probably the only book-length baseball poem in existence—and would react like a little leaguer to the rising and falling fortunes of the Athletics and the Phillies. He loved people, had many friends—some for several decades—and would treat a casual acquaintance to a discourse worthy of publication in a literary magazine.

In this love of life, love of beauty was paramount—

beauty of Nature, beauty in art, beauty of ideas, beauty of character. Thus, he traveled widely and enjoyed beautiful scenery, buildings, art works, stage productions, and music. He quickly passed over the ugly and the commonplace and always managed to find something that would kindle his ready enthusiasms. Yes, he loved life because he had the means and the ability to search out and enjoy the best it had to offer, and he was eager to share it with others through his conversations, lectures, and writings.

To conclude this biographical sketch nothing seems more fitting than Dr. Stork's own words, those used as his epitaph. They go far toward explaining why life was good and why he loved it: "There has been time for beauty, room for joy."

G. FREDERICK STORK
Chevy Chase, Maryland
February 1977

CHARLES WHARTON STORK CHRONOLOGY

1881 (February 12) born in Philadelphia

1898 graduated from Germantown Friends School, Philadelphia

1902 graduated from Haverford College

1903 M.A. from Harvard in English

1903-1905 Assistant in English at University of Pennsylvania

1904 "Arcades Ambo" (with R. M. Gummere)

1905 Ph.D. at University of Pennsylvania
study at Oxford England

1906-1908 Instructor in English at University of Pennsylvania

1907-1908 study at University of Munich

1908 married Elisabeth von Pausinger, daughter of Austrian artist Franz von Pausinger
"Day Dreams of Greece"

1909 first child, Rosalie, born

1910 "Plays of William Rowley" (edited)
"The Queen of Orplede"

1911 first son, Francis Wharton, born

1913 George Frederick born

1914 "The German Classics" (included English translations of a play and many poems)
took his family to visit the Pausingers in Saltzburg and due to war tension had difficulty getting back home to Philadelphia

1914-1916 Assistant Professor at University of Pennsylvania

1916 resigned his teaching position
"Sea and Bay: a Poem of New England"
"Selected Poems of Gustaf Fröding" (translated from Swedish)

1917 "Anthology of Swedish Lyrics from 1750 to 1915" (translation)
one-act play "Falstaff on Broadway" performed by the Plays and Players in Philadelphia

1917-1926 edited "Contemporary Verse" magazine (publication ended in 1929)

1918 "Lyrics of Hugo Von Hofmannsthal" (translated from German)

1919 "Sweden's Laureate" (translated poems of von Heidenstam)

1920 "Contemporary Verse Anthology"
"The Charles Men" (Swedish history by von Heidenstam—translation)
visit to Sweden

1922 "In the Sky Garden" (poems of S. M. Bird—edited)
decorated Order of Gustaf Vasa, First Class, by King Gustavas V of Sweden
wrote complete text (and read portions) of "Music and America: a Festival Performance with Music, Verse and Tableaux," performed by chorus and 80-piece orchestra

1923 "Second Contemporary Verse Anthology"
"Modern Swedish Masterpieces" (short story translations)
visit to Sweden

1924 "The Motherless" (novel by Bengt Berg—translated from Swedish)

1925 "The Swedes and Their Chieftains" (history by von Heidenstam—translation)

won Plays and Players contest with "The Flower Seller"

last child, Carl Alexander, born

1926 "The Flower Seller" performed by the Plays and Players

began one-year term as President of the Poetry Society of America

1927 became editor of "The Archer," international magazine of the Society of the Friends of Roerich

1928 "The Dragon and the Foreign Devils" (Chinese history by J. G. Anderson—translation from Swedish)

"Sweden's Best Stories" (translations, edited by H. A. Larsen)

1929 historical play "Ninon" performed in Hackensack, N. J.

President of the Society of the Friends of Roerich Museum

1930 "Martin Birck's Youth" (poems by Hjalmar Söderberg—translated from Swedish)

"Anthology of Swedish Lyrics" (translation)

1931 "I Sit Alone" (novel by W. Ager, translated from Norwegian)

1933 "Sunset Harbor": A Modern Idyll (novel)

1935 Began teaching at Harcum Junior College, Bryn Mawr, Pa.

"Short Stories of Hjalmar Söderberg" (translation)

1936 Play "Quaker Mother" performed off-Broadway, New York

1938 "Tales of Ensign Stål" (narrative poems by J. L. Runeberg, translated from Swedish)

"Arcadia B orealis" (poems of Axel Karlfeldt, translated from Swedish)

1939 visit to the Soviet Union and other European countries

"Sketches by an Athenian" (long poem describing his experience aboard the *Athenia* when it was torpedoed) published in the Saturday Evening Post

1942 "Anthology of Norwegian Lyrics" (translation) article on Swedish literature in "Collier's Encyclopedia"

1945, 1947 articles on Swedish literature in "Columbia Dictionary of Modern Literature"

1947 "A Second Book of Danish Verse" (supplemented and updated first book of translations by Damon and Hillyer)

1948 "On Board Old Ironsides: A Rope-Yarn Epic" crossed Pacific on carrier *Princeton*; visited China and India

1949 "Hearts and Voices" (poems about composers)

1950 visit to the Caribbean

1951 visit to South America

1952 "NAVPAC" (epic of the naval war in the Pacific)

1958 "A Vision of Misjudgment" (satire on modern poets)

1964 death of Carl Alexander Stork

1967 "Alcibiades" (historical play) published

1968 death of his wife

1971 (May 22) death

PUBLISHED WORKS OF
CHARLES WHARTON STORK (1881-1971)

POETRY

Arcades Ambo ("Arcadians Both," with Richard M. Gummere—poems inspired by the classics), W. H. Fisher and Co., Philadelphia, 1904

Day Dreams of Greece, J. B. Lippincott Co., Philadelphia, 1908

The Queen or Orplede (a romantic poem inspired by Mörike and other lyrics), J. B. Lippincott Co., Philadelphia, and Elkin Mathews, London, 1910

Sea and Bay: A Poem of New England (a book-length narrative poem), John Lane Co., New York, 1916

On Board Old Ironsides: A Rope-Yarn Epic (the story of a sailor on the *Constitution* in the War of 1812), Wing Press, Mill Valley, Calif., 1948

Hearts and Voices (poems about the great composers), Christopher Publishing House, Boston, 1949

NAVPAC (epic of the naval war in the Pacific), Bookman Associates, New York, 1952

PROSE

Sunset Harbor: A Modern Idyll (novel of a romance in a summer resort), Roland Swain Co., Philadelphia, 1933

A Vision of Misjudgment: An Adventure Among the Latest Poets (satire), Fine Editions Press, New York, 1958

DRAMA

Alcibiades: A Play of Athens in the Great Age, Syracuse University Press, Syracuse, N. Y., 1967

PROSE TRANSLATIONS

The Charles Men (Swedish history by Verner von Heidenstam), American-Scandinavian Foundation, New York, 1920

Modern Swedish Masterpieces (selected short stories), E. P. Dutton, New York, 1923

The Motherless (novel by Bengt Berg, from Swedish), Doubleday Page, Garden City, New York, 1924

The Swedes and Their Chieftains (history by Verner von Heidenstam), American-Scandinavian Foundation, New York, 1925

Sweden's Best Stories (ed. by H. A. Larsen and sponsored by the American-Scandinavian Foundation), W. W. Norton, New York, 1928

The Dragon and the Foreign Devils (Chinese history by J. G. Anderson), Little Brown, Boston, 1928

Martin Birck's Youth (selected short stories of Hjalmar Söderberg, from Swedish), Harper and Bros., New York and London, 1930

I Sit Alone (novel by Waldemar Ager, from Norwegian), Harper and Bros., New York and London, 1931

Short Stories of Hjalmar Söderberg (from Swedish), American-Scandinavian Foundation, New York, 1935

BOOKS EDITED

Plays of William Rowley (Ph.D. thesis), Published for the University (of Pennsylvania), Philadelphia, 1910

Contemporary Verse Anthology (selected poems from the pages of *Contemporary Verse* magazine), E. P. Dutton, New York, 1920

In the Sky Garden (poems of Stephen Moylan Bird), Yale Univ. Press, New Haven, 1922

Second Contemporary Verse Anthology, E. P. Dutton, New York, 1923

The German Classics (translations of a play and many poems in a twenty volume set of books edited by Kuno Francke), German Publication Society, New York, 1913-1914

Selected Poems of Gustaf Fröding (from Swedish), Macmillan, New York, 1916

Anthology of Swedish Lyrics from 1790 to 1950, American-Scandinavian Foundation, New York; Humphrey Milford, London; and Oxford Univ. Press, 1917. Revised and republished 1930

Lyrics of Hugo von Hofmannsthal (from German), Yale Univ. Press, New Haven, 1918

Sweden's Laureate (poems of Verner von Heidenstam), Yale Univ. Press, New Haven; Humphrey Milford, London; and Oxford Univ. Press, 1919

Tales of Ensign Stål (poems of J. L. Runeberg, translated from Swedish), Princeton Univ. Press, Princeton, N. J., 1938

Arcadia Borealis (poems of Erik Axel Karlfeldt, translated from Swedish), Univ. of Minnesota Press, Minneapolis, Minn., 1938

Anthology of Norwegian Lyrics (sponsored by the American-Scandinavian Foundation), Princeton Univ. Press, Princeton; Humphrey Milford, London; and Oxford Univ. Press, 1942. Reissued by Books for Libraries Press, Freeport, N. Y., 1968

A Second Book of Danish Verse (updates the first book by S. F. Damon and R. S. Hillyer), Princeton Univ. Press, Princeton, 1947. Reissued by Books for Libraries Press, Freeport, N. Y., 1968.

NOTES AND ACKNOWLEDGMENTS

"Forget Not Beauty" (page 26) : published in *The New Yorker*

"To Stones from a New England Beach" (page 36) : published in the *Vineyard Gazette* May 1, 1964

"June" (page 41) : orginally entitled "Fanfare for a Royal Progress" and published in a newspaper; set to music by G. Frederick Stork in solo and mixed chorus arrangements

"Standards" (page 48) : in *The Nation* June 15, 1918, and also in a literature textbook

"A Painter in New England" (page 50) : from *Sea and Bay* (see Bibliography)

"Early Morning by a Lake" (page 53) : published in *Wings*, a quarterly poetry magazine

"A Mountain Lake at Twilight (page 54) : published in *Wings*

"Sea Song" (page 55) : set to music for chorus by Robert Flagler and published

"The Two Untamed" (page 56) : published in the *Forum* and reprinted in the *Christian Advocate* February 4, 1926; set to music by G. Frederick Stork for baritone solo and for mixed chorus

"Fish Course" (page 59) : published in *The Diplomat*

"Sketches by an 'Athenian' " (page 64) : published in *The Saturday Evening Post* November 4, 1939; a first-hand account of Dr. Stork's experience when the British luxury liner *Athenia* was torpedoed on September 2, 1939

"To Paul Daugherty" (page 77) : describes a three-by-four-foot oil painting owned by Dr. Stork, now in the possession of his son Francis

"Sea Painting by Albert Ryder" (page 78) : published in *The Diplomat*; describes a counterfeit Ryder painting owned by Francis

"The Joy of Effort" (page 80) : published in *American Sonnets and Lyrics*

The frontispiece color slide of Dr. Stork was taken at Martha's Vineyard about 1946. The endpaper scene, entitled "New England Nocturne," shows Menemsha Harbor on an evening in August 1962. Both photographs were taken by G. Frederick Stork. The drawing of Gay Head and the lighthouse was by Cathy Stork, one of Dr. Stork's grandchildren.

The selection of poems and the planning of this volume have been a joint effort of the three surviving children of Dr. Stork: Mrs. Rosalie Regen, Francis W. Stork, and G. Frederick Stork. The task could not have been accomplished without the cooperation of The Athenæum of Philadelphia and the invaluable assistance of its Secretary and Librarian, Dr. Roger W. Moss, Jr. Thanks are also due to Walnut Grove Associates for the great care which they devoted to the design and production of the book.

The manuscripts and correspondence files of Dr. Stork have been deposited at The Athenæum of Philadelphia, East Washington Square, Philadelphia, Pennsylvania 19106, where they may be consulted upon application. A few similar papers, donated before his death, are in the library at Syracuse University.

The Poems

Forget Not Beauty

Forget not beauty, lest she pass you by
And leave you as she found you. Set your heart
In ambush at the loophole of your eye;
Unsought she comes, unhindered must depart.
She does not flaunt, she does not cry her wares;
She slips along in silence, makes no stir.
Yours is the chance, the choice; she never cares—
Your interest, your neglect are one to her.
For all that, she is seldom far away.
Forget her not, be patient for a while,
And when at last you meet her, bid her stay
A moment, till the impact of her smile
    Full on your heart unseals its hidden springs
    And makes it tremble as at touch of wings.

Song of Gratitude

The sea wind is a gentle wind
Tonight, tonight;
No restless urge to fret the mind,
The spirit to excite.

I love you, wind, just as you are.
My need is deep.
I bless you; under yon tranquil star
You waft me to my sleep.

Menemsha Inlet

What is so calm and sweet and blest
As a little harbor with boats at rest:
Racers and launches and fishing craft,
Swimmers that splash from a leaning raft,
Smooth reflections of rock and tree,
And out past the narrows a glimpse of sea?
While I, of the scene a conscious part,
Have a harbor for all in my welcoming heart.

A Seaside Lake in Summer

It is a lonely lake;
Few houses dent the shoreline,
And seldom a canoe steals gliding by.
Often toward twilight
We slip down through the bushes to the lake
And let it sink into our thought.
So lonely it is,
So intimate, so undemanding,
It seems to crave our sympathy,
And yet it has its own inherent life,
Especially with the birds.

A flight of swallows dips and veers,
Mirrored in its placidity.
We cannot hear them,
Yet we feel sure they twitter to each other
In lively gossiping.
How different the white, slow-circling gulls,
With steady wingbeats,
Powerful, impressive,
Plodding, it almost could be said of them,
And harsh of voice, unsociable.
The loons—they don't come often—
Are even more aloof, but never stolid.

They have a charm of wildness that enchants us;
Dark velvet with flecks of white, as a field-glass tell us,
On the unrippling silver of the lake,
In twos and threes they calmly sit and drift,
So shy, so restful.
The heron, standing still among the reeds,
Is always alone, not idle, concentrating.
Etched black against low clouds,
A wedge of duck drives purposefully past
And seldom pauses.
A hawk swerves back and forth around the clumps
Of bayberry and dwarf pines.
But the most dramatic sight of all
Is when a score of noble Canada geese,
Diverted from their long flight to the south,
Choose here their resting place.
Proudly they settle and with dignity
Dispose themselves to forage.
They are like English lords, correctly dressed
For dinner in their black and white and gray.
Even when they dip their beaks to feed,
Exposing glints of fluffy tails,
They cannot seem indecorous.
Once, memorably, an otter came,
And we for weeks through glasses watched
Him dive, lie on his back, and otherwise
Disport himself.

And yet the lake is not mere passive background;
It has a gaiety of its own.
Its slender reeds and tufted grasses
Are delicately patterned
Against the silver ripples, as they sway
To the soft impulse of a languid breeze.
Bright water flowers in clusters
Rise boldly from the shore:
Tall, pointed loosestrife
With purple knots of tiny blossom
Set close around its spires.
Around them thread the dragonflies,
Thick black, thin blue.
In August the pink mallows loop the bank
With crinoline flounces.

It is not special times of day
Or changes of the season
That most endear you to us, lonely lake.
Like Cleopatra, with her infinite variety,
You fascinate, enthral us.
Ever since boyhood days the open ocean
Has with a ruling passion claimed me;
There never has been a more compelling surge
Of rapture in my soul
Than when across its deep blue boundlessness
I span its vast horizon,
Or when I buffet through its crashing breakers
And from their hollows gaze up at the sky.

Yet now, grown older,
Often I'm glad to shift into this new
Delight, this harbor of declining years
That infinite nature opens to her children.
I shall not ever tire of you, kind lake,
Of that I am sure.

By day, by night, in tempest or in calm
I watch the changing lights and shades that pass
And vivify your beauty.
You glass the flowers and trees, the birds and clouds,
The dawns, the noons, the sunsets and the stars.
Whenever I gaze at you or think of you,
In heart and mind and body I respond
As to the greeting of a cherished friend.
You have a constancy in all your moods
That I can base my faith on.

A lake is lonely, but when loneliness
Is filled so to the brim with teeming life,
With color and with motion, is it strange
To find in it an open sesame
Of heartening comradeship and quiet joy?

Evening on Martha's Vineyard

A Panel Sketch

Up in the west,
A brightening star
Floats lone and clear.
Below it, to the right,
The new moon sickles through
A thin, pale scarf of violet cloud,
While from beyond the curve of nearby hills
And distant, level dunes
The firm vermilion pencil of the afterglow
Sets at the bottom of the scroll
Its proud imperial signature.

The Ancient Dunes

The years have built and whittled at these dunes,
The light green blades of swordgrass curve and flash,
And through a myriad myriads of noons
Untiringly the wave-mounds rear and crash.

Nothing is here to tempt the lust of man
To break the spell of Beauty's free domain,
Where all things are as when they first began
And as they have been ever shall remain.

Beach Pebbles

Alice and Trina are two friends of mine.
We bathe together in the seething brine.
I breast the waves, they splash along the shore;
I don't know which of us enjoys it more.
Just lately I've been taken with the notion
Of gathering pebbles tossed up by the ocean.
Many are beautiful and strange to me.
Most grown-up folks, I'm sure, would not agree.
Alice and Trina, though, to my surprise,
Exclaimed and studied them with wondering eyes,
And when I told them each could have her choice,
Announced their pleasure almost with one voice.
Alice picked out a humped one with the glow
Of marble, white as pure, unmelting snow.
Then Trina took a flat one like a locket
That just would fit into her jersey pocket.
What she liked most in it was the starry glint
Of mica silver on its soft brown tint;
I was so happy with them, as I thought:
Here they have treasures that cannot be bought.
These pebbles were the playthings of the sea.
The waves grew tired and left them here for me.
My friends will often look at them and feel
That they have something shining, smooth and real,
And though the truth can hardly be expressed,
They'll know that nature's toys are still the best.

To Stones from a New England Beach

Millenniums old, what strange vicissitudes,
Had sight been yours, you must have seen before
You found repose here. Lapidary moods
May well be hard to fathom, yet the lore
Of your adventures is a tempting theme
To dwell on. In the lonely dim abyss
Of time you underwent the age of fire
And then of ice, mad heat and cold extreme,
Then ocean's wrath before you came to this,
Tossed on the beach, sans motion, sans desire.

We fancy you impervious to all feeling.
Perhaps it may not be so. Who is free
To judge? For as I look, a slow revealing
Tells that we have a kinship, you with me.
The tie is hidden, yet is surely there;
It is no fiction of a careless mind.
My bones are stone—I do not count them dead.
How would my brains, my sprawling vitals fare
Without a firmly-fitted frame to bind
A shield for them, a holding-place, a bed?

Long have I gathered, looked at you and felt you,
Until I pierced below your crude uncouthness.
It seemed as if my passionate thought could melt you,
Delighting in your color, pattern, smoothness.
Here was a beauty mystic, depthless, pure,
As of the sea, the mountains and the stars,
Unlike the loveliness of trees and flowers,
A self-reliance, potent to endure
Through all the wear of changefulness that mars
The fading victims of the withering hours.

I learned to prize you, stones, not in a mass,
But separately, until you came to be
No jumble for the cold eye to assess,
But each with its own personality.
Some I admired for pleasing shades of color:
Soft orange-brown, or bolder black on white,
Pale pink or green, rich purple, delicate mauve.
It's true without your sea-gleam you were duller,
Yet bold in character still, though not so bright,
And hardly less to me a treasure trove.

You had the dignity of age as well,
And so were suited for companionship
With one whose youth was memory. I could dwell
In harmony with you, despite the slip
Of bygone years that leave more than they take.
And there's a sort of gaiety in you,
Braving the swirl and grind of generations,
For in your texture there is many a flake,
As of the finest silver, minted new
And crusted thick in tiny constellations.

Some of you I have chosen for symmetry
And others for their pattern. Nature still
Is art's first teacher, and the sooner we
Grant that, the sooner we may prove our skill.
What is it that wise Nature most demands
Of him who feels the impulse to create
A something out of chaos? Not the flair
Of fame-lust, but the toil of patient hands,
Of love, thought-disciplined to consecrate
Its fullest powers. To labor is to dare.

Nature is opulent, lavish, prodigal;
Her gifts are not to us of equal worth.
We must select what we can use of all
Her bounties to evolve a different birth.
So was it with you, stones. I sorted out
Of hundreds this one here and that one there.
Why, I could hardly tell. I found a meaning
Others might laugh at, sometimes was in doubt
Which was irrelevant, which to me was rare.
Such was the curious method of my gleaning.

Though I made friends with those of you I kept,
I thought of you most often as a whole.
There was a divine significance that slept
Within you, but would wake: you had a soul.
That soul a Michelangelo could feel,
Could bring to life. And Moses' laws of old
Were written on your tablets. Shakespeare found
Sermons in you, 'Twas said that you could heal;
That men were made from you, Greek legend told,
And that you sang, gave forth a lovely sound.

Stones were held sacred, cavil as one may.
The tales of science are as strange, though true.
In sober earnest once again I say
There's an affinity between me and you,
My doughty comrades, eloquent with more
Than words. The same Creator made us both
To be, and be together. I rejoice
In what you have added to my cherished store
Of beauty, and I thank you, nothing loath.
You speak to me, and I have heard your voice.

June

Are you near now? Give us warning,
June;
Will you burst on us one morning
Soon?
Dearly, deeply as we love you,
Could we bear the sweetness of you,
All your weight of leaf and flower
Tumbled on us in an hour?
You must give us ample warning,
June.

From too sudden rapture spare us,
June;
Send the tulips to prepare us,
June.
When their crimson trumpets stutter,
Purple iris pennons flutter;
All in robe of golden flame you
Come; all nature will acclaim you
Summer's bride and springtime's heiress,
June!

Summer Ecstasy

Out on the ocean
The lesser waves dance
With silvery joy
In the sun's broad glance,

While the surf's white regiments
Charge, retreat,
Timed with the throb
Of their drum's dull beat.

Over the yielding
Pale marsh grasses
The quick, soft hand
Of a wind gust passes.

But up in the high blue,
Firm, never drifting,
The cloudland's Himalayan
Ramparts are lifting.

Each of the moods
Alike is blest:
Unending motion,
Eternal rest.

Sketch in Perspective

Martha's Vineyard, Mid-September

The pale pastel
Of light green meadow weeds,
Enwoven on the pinkish mat
Of withered grass stems
And thickly dotted with the salt-white discs
Of Queen Anne's lace.
Behind it, just across a gray stone wall,
The somber dignity of swamp-land thicket,
Mantled in goldenrod,
Into which cuts a purple scythe of pond
Bordered with brown-topped reeds.
Last, on the horizon, chalky streaks of dune
Open their mounded battlements
In blue embrasures to the level sea.

Leaf-Mould

What's the chief charm of woods—besides mere trees?
Not tang of balsam; not the gray-voiced croon
Of pine-harps, with a bird-call flashing bold
Against it; not the fingered light on moss
And flowers that play "I spy," courted in turn
By bourgeois bees and foppish butterflies;
Not rabbits dodging with their fluffy tails,
Or the striped chipmunks either, jauntily
Rehearsing family secrets. No, I think
It's leaf-mould. Only fancy if the trail
Were asphalt, or macadam! Leaf-mould gives
The heartbeat of the mystery, all the sap
And vigor of centuries underneath your soles
At every buoyant motion. Stretch your thighs
And run your bravest, leaping root and stone,
Rising and plunging on the mounded trail
To float as on delicious tropic waves.
So will the leaf-mould be transformed again
To living rapture. Leaf-mould, damp and dark,
The wreck of woodland life—you vent a sigh,
For the lost green and gold, the frail slain flowers,
For balm dispersed, for happy songsters dumb
With unrecorded fame; but from this mould
Is born new wonder: fragrance, color, song,
All freshly woven by the patient years.
When I tread leaf-mould, dark thrill of strength
And awe speaks through me like a tactile voice:
"Here is perennial joy fed rich on death."

The Veil of Fog

I can give welcome to a foggy day
As freely, for the freshness of its change,
As to the bravest blue and gold display
That sunlight ever blazoned. Is that strange?
The softened brown, dim purple, muted green
Whisper their secret to me in a smile
With finger on the lips, more felt than seen,
The childlike reticence of innocent guile.
The deepest joys of life, that most endure,
Are half concealed within a floating veil,
Awaiting our discovery. Crystal pure,
Outlasting time, their truth can never fail.
    So does the fog instil the urge in me
    To vision what no outward eye can see.

Nirvana

When the thin clouds melt
In the warm noon sky,
Where do they go?
Where do you and I?

They dwell unseen
In the peace of blue.
Why not as well then
I and you?

Clouds at Midnight

The sweep of the clouds o'er the face of the night
Is a tumult of terror and splendor in flight,
So silent, so weightless, so proud and so vast,
As the folds of their banner drive billowing past.
Oh, the swiftness, the wild headlong joy of the scene,
With the pale frightened moon peering vaguely between!

The fond race of mortals, how vainly they boast
Of their pitiful feats in the realm of the air,
Their toy planes and bombs. Let them look at the host
Above them and vaunt of themselves if they dare!
Aye, let them behold, like the psalmist of yore,
The chariots of God whirling wrathful to war!

Standards

White is the skimming gull on the somber green of the
    fir-trees;
Black is the soaring gull on a snowy glimmer of cloud.

The Elder Sacrament

Past this meadow on the shore
Glinting seagulls dip and soar.
Boats festoon the purple bay;
And out beyond its rim of gray,
Languid in the August sheen,
Mountain ridges, dusky green
As some faded tapestry,
Drowse at full length opposite me.
Soft across the sky of noon
Folds of thinnest cloud are strewn,
Blurring the hardness of its hue
Till blue is white and white is blue.
Then as the veils above me shift,
So my senses drift and drift,
Lost beyond the will to think,
Motionless I eat and drink.

Lord of love and truth and power,
Thou art with me in this hour,
For Thy spirit is not lent
To a church-walled sacrament
More than to the simpler food
Of an open solitude;
And Thy rich outpouring grace
Fills this beauty-hallowed place,
Showing here Thy flesh indeed
And Thy blood to slake man's need
Freely given for all to share—
Bread of earth and wine of air.

A Painter in New England

Did you ever note the beauty of the soft
    New England grasses,
  All the ochres, reds and browns?
And the flowers: the purple asters and the
    goldenrods' rich masses,
  With the cardinals' flaming gowns,
Dots of blood against the tangle of the reedy,
    lone morasses,
Where the nodding cattails rustle under
    every wind that passes.
  Ah! what reticent depth of color,
  Growing brighter, growing duller,
As a smile of sunlight broadens or a brow of
    storm-cloud frowns!

Have you read the blazoned glory of the
    sunset's revelations
  Glowing scarlet streaked with gold?
Have you seen the sky-towers crumbling in
    stupendous conflagrations,
  Passing gorgeous to behold,
While the East is hung with tapestries in
    dove-serene gradations,
And the naked vault of heaven is filled with
    rosy undulations?
  Where in all the world resplendent
  Or the poet's mind transcendent
Can such miracles be rivaled, form so grand
    or hue so bold?

Have you watched the dreamy progress of
        a gray New England schooner
    Drifting seaward with the tide
Darkly down a lane of radiance, dawn-lit
        gold or silvery lunar,
    Ribbon-narrow or ocean-wide?
Such a boat in such a background I will paint
        you ten times sooner
Than a lily-perfect yacht with drooping top-
        sail and ballooner.
    No, for me the old-time vessel
    In a land-locked bay to nestle
Till the light wind flaps her staysail and the
        light wave laps her side.

Have you shrunk before the grimness of the
        rugged longshore ledges
    Where the groundswell surf rolls in
Round the battlemented coastline with its
        walls and bastion wedges?
    Hark! the cave-resounding din,
As a breaker smites the granite with the
        strength of giant sledges,
And a swaying fringe of foam enfolds the
        rampart's dripping edges.
    Lovely lands across the ocean
    Thrill the heart with quick emotion,
But the shore of staid New England holds
        a rapture hard to win.

The Roots of the Birch

Look at the birch on the grim cliff's edge.
How can it hold to that perilous ledge
When the gales of winter come slashing down,
Piling the drifts on its delicate crown:
So slender its trunk, so frail each bough
That rustles in August breezes now?

Ah! but look at the roots there, strong
As twisted pythons, that reach along
The face of the rock till they find a hold
Deep down under the mossy mold;
Thick they are as the trunk of the tree,
And firm as only roots can be.

"Tis thus, O Beauty, that thou shouldst grow,"
Slender and fair, but held below
By tense, rough roots that have learned to clasp
The living rock with an iron grasp.
Nerved to the onslaught of wind and snow—
"Tis thus, O Beauty, that thou shouldst grow."

Early Morning by a Lake

Earth's breast has caught a vision of the sky
And holds it to her heart. The white and blue
That intermingles for a mortal eye
To welcome, awe-struck at a scene so new
It passes comprehension—how can thought
Seek to convey what now entrances me?
It is not tranquil water that has wrought
This miracle of light and purity.
As I look down, a portal opens wide
Below me that uncovers to the gaze
Another world in splendor glorified,
Lovelier than all above it, past all praise.
   I could not ask for more. The truth shines clear;
   Heaven is not far or doubtful; it is here.

A Mountain Lake at Twilight

Two worlds in one : the upper outlined clear
And sharp as truth, the other soft and blurred
Or broken ; gentle Nature's arms engird
A mirror where her features disappear.
Smoothest at twilight the reflection here,
Yet even now the silver may be stirred
By the wing-feathers of a dipping bird
Or when a fish leaps like a hurtling spear.

But pine-dark shore, gray cliffs and deepening blue
Are fixed ; the water soon again will take
Their image, be again their counterpart.
In the calm joy of beauty, what was two
Is blended indivisibly. This lake—
Is it the outward world or my own heart?

Sea Song

I have lent myself to thy will, O Sea!
    To the urge of thy tidal sway;
My soul to thy lure of mystery,
    My cheek to thy lashing spray.
        For there's never a man whose blood runs warm
        But would quaff the wine of the brimming storm.
    As the prodigal lends, have I lent to thee
        For a day or a year and a day.

And what if the tale be quickly told
    And the voyage be wild and brief?
I can face thy fury with courage bold
    And never a whine of grief,
        Though peril-fanged is thy grisly track,
        The ship goes out that never comes back,
    And the sailor's whitened bones are rolled
        In the surge of the whitening reef.

The shores recede, the great sails fill,
    The lee rail hisses under,
As we double the cape of Lighthouse Hill
    Where sea and harbor sunder.
        Then here's to a season of glad unrest!
        With an anchor of home on the seaman's breast,
    Till I claim once more from thy savage will
        A soul that is fraught with wonder.

The Two Untamed

You may conquer the plain with plough and drain
    And the forest with axe and saw.
You may pierce the hills with power drills
    And shatter the mountain's awe.
But there are two you will not subdue,
    Though you curb however you can;
They will brave the test of your worst and best—
    The sea and the heart of man.

The desert may yield as a watered field,
    And the wind may grind your grain,
The river's might may be yoked in light
    Or tug at a factory chain.
But muscle nor mind these two can bind
    By cunningest plot or plain;
They shall have free play to the Judgment Day—
    The sea and the heart of man.

You may note their deeds and guess at the creeds
    That govern their ebb and flow;
There are tales to tell why their passions swell,
    But the secret you never will know.
And, willing or loath, you must love them both,
    Though heaven alone may span
And fathom the breast of their deep unrest—
    The sea and the heart of man.

Breakers on a Windless Morning

These breakers are like minutes of the hours
When you are happy-thoughtful and at peace.
Gently their emerald beauty rears and flowers,
While best of all is that they never cease.
They reassure me with their measured motion
As with a certitude that will not fail,
Making a garden of the desolate ocean.
Wild though they seem, there must a law prevail
Over their tossing crests. They roam afar,
But they are bound into a cosmic plan
That rules the light-waves of the distant star
And guides the doubtful destiny of man.
    We, too, are waves upon a greater sea,
    Are we not made as we were meant to be?

Seaweeds

These delicate little tufts and streamers,
Like floating bouquets
Caught in the rhythms of the cool green water—
With what a grace of changing patterns
They spread their tendrils,
Dark brown, pale olive, coral pink;
To watch them is a joy.
If I should take them in my hand,
They would be ugly, meaningless, inert.
I let them stay where they belong,
Untouched.

Fish Course

Broiled Spanish Mackerel

An oily tarnished oblong barred with black . . .
Palmettos flaunt above a Florida key,
And a lithe spear-shape with a green gold back
Tears a white foam-wound through the purple sea.

Cold Salmon

A slab of pink, sliced lemon on the dish . . .
Under a Canada moon the dark pines dream,
And like a rocket—look! A silver fish
Breasts the wild fury of the tumbling stream.

Stewed Halibut

What's here? A sauce-besmothered hunk of white . . .
Far down below the North Atlantic's roar
A quaint, flat monster like a headlong kite
Lunges through ice-green depths off Labrador.

Flying-Fish: An Ode

Low lies Bermuda on our starboard bow;
The morning's hue is misty like a pearl's,
As lightly through the severing swells we plough;
To right and left the widening foam-wedge curls.
I stand and watch alone:
No slanting sail, no black and stalwart hull,
Not even one stray gull
To fleck the languid ocean's monotone;
Nothing but sky and sea
And, vague with mystery,
Yon distant island, fairy-like, unknown.

But what is that? Scarce fifty yards away
A flock of birds where bird before was none,
Skimming across the smooth unlustrous gray
On wings that glint so oddly in the sun.
No sooner seen than lost,
Melted like scudding snowflakes as they touch
The surface, not so much
As one black bobbing head of all that host.
Yet see! once more they rise
And, like strange dragonflies,
Along our bow-flung breakers deftly coast.

At last I know you, birds that may not soar,
Shuttlers between two elements. Your flight
So low, so little veering, and the four
Short filmy wings that, quivering, catch the light—
These told me what you were.
Audacious truants from your parent sea,
Half fabulous are ye,
O flashing ones, O sylph-like beings rare,
That, heedless quite of earth,
Spring toward a nobler birth
From the dim waters to the radiant air!

How must it be to swim among your kind,
Dull with the cold and dreary with the dark,
Enclosed above, beneath, before, behind
In green uncertainty, from which a shark
At any time may dash
And doom you like some huge demonic fate
With lust insatiate?
He cuts the water with a seething gash.
What use to dart aside?
Those great jaws, grinning wide,
Will close your frolic as the long teeth clash.

But I forget your gift: the bonds that hold
The others of your race are loosed for you,
For you alone. The silver dolphin bold
Shoots like a spray-haired comet from the blue,
But may not poise or flit
As you do—. What if but a minute's space?
Hardly a longer grace
Has poet, saint or lover. Nor a whit
Less sure to sink are we;
Our wings of ecstasy
No loftier, no longer joy permit.

Yet joy it is! To scorn the dread of death,
To dwell for shining moments in the sun
Of Beauty and sweet Love, to drink one breath
Of a diviner element—though but one;
To reach a higher state
Of being, to explore a new domain;
To leap, and leap again,
Unheeding the gray menace of our fate
That follows till we fall:
For—fishes, men and all—
The grim old Shark will have us, soon or late.

Then tell me, comrades, does your little flight
Thrill with the foretaste of a life to be?
Is your ethereal revel in the light
The promise of some fair eternity,
Where you may roam at will,
Safe from the terror of the world you knew,
On wings of rainbow hue?
How vain to question! I may ask my fill.
One life is all you wish;
You fly, and are but fish;
Your gift, a trick of blind instinctive skill.

And I who ask—what certainty is mine
That these poor flights (which seemingly exalt
My soul into an element more fine)
Foretell me immortality?—I halt.
Then from the depths of dread
Once more my faith-winged spirit flashes free
And quaffs eternity!

     .   .   .   .   .   .

I start and look: the flying-fish have fled,
Have got them to their kind,
Or tamely dropped behind.
The ship drives on; Bermuda looms ahead.

Sketches by an "Athenian"

I. Premonition

August the twenty-fifth, Southampton Harbor.
Our tender, luggage-piled, steals nosing out
Through straw-gold mist
To meet the *Hansa*.
All kinds of boats we pass;
Liners and tramps and tugs and barges.
Well out into the Solent
Beyond the shore boats,
We peer and peer.
What's that big hull?
A burly battle cruiser.
Yonder's a lean destroyer. There's another.
The watchdogs are on duty.
But where's the *Hansa?*
She sailed from Hamburg yesterday.
We pause and drift, bright sunlight overhead.
Gentle and graceful as a flock of doves,
A fleet of racing knockabouts
Goes slipping by us.
We drift and drift.
It's getting late. We question and conjecture.
Our radio has no contact with the *Hansa*.
A group of us take lunch.
Still drifting.
Then we turn back.
In Southampton they tell us that the *Hansa*
Has been recalled to Hamburg.
That looks—well, not so good.

II. Interlude

So back to London.
A hectic morning, but by great good luck
I get a cabin on the *Athenia*
To sail September second.
What's to be done this long unwelcome week?
A friend invites me for a day in Sussex.
We climb the Downs, those rippling greyhound backs
That ridge the countryside.
The towers of Lewes Castle are behind us,
Quaint little hamlets nestle at our feet
Around their churches,
Sheep dot the upland pastures,
And grain fields glint below them,
With dark irregular woodland splotched between.
The springy turf is rich with tiny flowers;
Blue scabious, orange trefoil,
And suddenly a great pink-purple patch
Of heather flames the gorse.
Far to the south we glimpse the turquoise Channel.
This landscape was the scene of many wars;
Briton and Roman, Saxon, Dane and Norman;
Here nobles fought with kings, and Catholics
With Protestants, and Cavaliers with Roundheads.
But peace returned, and peace is here today.
A zooming airplane hurtles silverly
Above us, and we shiver;
Then peace and silence and soft loveliness
Flow back.

III. Cold Murder

Swaddled in luxury, we pace the deck.
We got off just in time.
Sunday, the third, we hear of war declared,
But that's behind us now;
America will certainly look good.
We still must take precautions, all lights out
For two more days, and boat drill—that's all right,
No doubt.
Seated at Sunday dinner, half past seven.
How good the food is! "A *coupe Jacques,*
Please, waiter."
I'm talking with a lady on my right.

A crash, high-pitched and hellish, frigid steel!
Blackness!
A sick slow lurch to port
(As if pushed down by a relentless hand)
Of the poor stricken thing
That just the millionth of a second ago
Was a brave ship.
These three—the least, alone, too terrible
For thought at such a time—and all at once.
We are not frightened; there are no hysterical screams;
We are appalled.

Death fronts us, looks us level in the brain,
While in the dark we hear the tables slide
And china crash.
A small hand is in mine,
A woman's voice is murmuring anxiously
Something, "If I could only get to my friend!"
And I say, "Keep your head!"
There's very little noise.
I've time to think,
"Those Germans may be devils, but they're smart.
They got the jump on England."
We make our way out toward the stairway,
Lighted by matches that the stewards hold.
Our whistle is blowing the signal, "To the boats!"
I reach my room, get down a life preserver,
Start out, run back and take my overcoat,
Then climb to the upper deck.
They're getting the boats out there already.

What was it? Nobody knows.
An infernal machine?
The poor *Athenia* staggers like a groggy boxer.
The first boats are in the water. Women go down
To them on rope ladders. They push off.
The other boats take much longer to get clear.
Then only one is left.
There's a bit of a panic, nothing very much.
The rest of us pile right into her as she hangs.
I am the last aboard.
It's crowded, but not desperately.
They start to lower us.
This is bad.

A slip —— Mustn't think. . . .
We jerk down, pretty evenly so far.
I don't remember till our stern strikes water,
Setting off wild, thin, foreign-sounding screams.
What are these women in the boat with me?
The bow comes down. We push or drift away.
Ah! So we're safe, if you can call it safe
To be in an open rowboat far from land
In darkness with a sea that runs to waves
Five feet above our gunwales.
But we have word from the *Athenia's* deck
A rescue ship will come in half an hour.

IV. Moonlight on the Atlantic

Ten or so men and sixty women and children.
We get out oars, but all that we can do
Is steady her a bit.
I tell them there'll be moonlight before long.
We catch a glimpse of other boats and hail them;
Then a pale ghost light flares on the *Athenia*
As on a death-drained cheek.
It's chilly, but not cold.
Time passes, and we talk.
Several on board have seen the submarine
Half hidden by her gun smoke,
Have seen the shattered upper deck
And bodies covered in tarpaulins
That dripped with red.
We are too busy at our heavy rowing
To take much notice.
Our tub rides well;
It's only once a wave crest splashes in.

Odd, inarticulate sounds rise quavering
From the thick-huddled women in the stern;
They're Poles and Germans, mostly, from the steerage.
Then with a wide imperial sweep of the arm
The lavish moonlight sows the gloomy furrows
With living beauty.
A group of us Americans
Sing "Sweet and Low."
It's very quiet now,
Two little girls near me seem to be asleep.
Lights rise, approach. The rescue ship!
Soon comes another.
We drift quite close to one, yelling, "Ship ahoy!"
Then past into the dark,
The moon being in a cloud.
Stars, though, are clear; Orion low is in the east.
To north a delicate play of northern lights
Flickers its spectral fires below the Dipper.
Moonlight again.
The rescue ships are far away,
So, too, the *Athenia.*
We burn a red flare.
An old Scotch woman mutters hopelessly,
"Ye don't think we can be saved?"
"We're practically saved already."
I say it and don't dare not to think it.

V. H.M.S. Escort

Dawn, clear, superb,
Flushing vast battlements of cloud.
Six ships around us:
A white yacht, a big freighter,
Three gray destroyers and the *Athenia,*
Looking as high in the water as when we left her.
Empty white lifeboats bob among the crests.
We chorus out a treble "Ship ahoy!"
When one of the destroyers comes our way,
But she veers off again.
Suspense.
The other boats, it seems, are all picked up.
We can't, we can't have been unnoticed;
And yet——
No, like a sea archangel, sweeping down,
The last destroyer comes.
My heart swells, but the fearful wash of the waves
Against her side is agony to look at.
Ropes are flung out to us, caught; rope ladders hang
Before us. "Come ahead! No hurry!"
A petty officer with carroty hair
And a chin strap superintends—
The tears start when I think of what we owe him.
We get the children and women to the ladders,
The sailors pull them up.
With some of the older women we fit a rope
Under their life belts,
And they are swung straight in.

We work too fast to think, until
The women and children are all safely up.
It's our turn. Now it's mine!
There is a ghastly surge, high up to the deck
Almost, then a ten-foot drop.
I'm set to jump. . . . Thank God, I didn't.
The jerk would have torn me off.
On the next upswell I get on the ladder.
My muscles only serve to keep my hold.
I'm pulled up, caught by the shoulders, dragged aboard.

VI. Second Interlude

If there are any finer men alive
Than British tars, I never hope to see them;
Gentle as women, full of kind attentions,
And gay as schoolboys on a picnic.
We hear of terrible things:
All the men killed in the engine room,
A lifeboat cut in two by the freighter's propeller,
Drowned bodies of women and children,
Only six saved.
The U-boat tried to shoot away our wireless.
If that's not murder ——
The poor *Athenia's* still afloat
We're going to sink her, but as we come abreast,
She starts to go of herself.
Her stern is under, then her bow tilts up,
Shows red, and down she slides.
Well, there goes my new dinner-jacket suit
And a signed photograph of Sibelius.

I sleep six hours,
Wake up, have a bite to eat, get out on deck.
A sailor plays a mouth organ;
He plays it with the spirit of a Kreisler;
A group of American college girls,
Bedraggled, but still charming,
Applaud and sing.
We slip along delightfully.
Next morning up on deck again at sunrise.
We're bound for Glasgow,
And soon the shoulders of great Highland crags
Rise dark and rugged from a cloak of mist.
Seven destroyers in a line skim past us.
Why not have given us one of them as a convoy
Night before last?
We go ashore at Greenock.
A weary wait; at last a motorbus
Takes us to Glasgow and a good Scotch breakfast.
Howard A. Bowman, the American consul—
God bless him, his good wife and son forever!—
Takes me to his home;
And three days later, thanks to him, I'm off
On the *Wacosta*, freighter, once again.

VII. Meeting a Gentleman

Under the Stars and Stripes.
No blackouts now, we floodlight flag and shields
Along our sides.
The simple life, plain food and bunks in the hold.
Just after midday dinner
The second day out, not far from where
The *Athenia* sank—
"Bang!"
We're not hit this time, but a submarine
Is out in full view on the starboard bow,
Twinkling electric signals.
We stop and run up flags.
"Good glory, haven't I had my full-sized share
Of submarines already?"
Still, if she's signaling, she doesn't mean
To blow us up straight off.
The other passengers are all on deck,
So I stay with them,
Not any too happy.
Remembering stories back in 1812,
I think they'll make us send a boat to fetch
An officer aboard.
They do. The sub goes round to windward of us,
The sun behind her.
Look at her conning tower, a sharp black notch
Against the silver waves;
Her men silhouetted thick along her back,
Glad of the air, no doubt!

The light streams filtering through the small round holes
In bow and stern,
Speckling the foam.
God! What a fascinating devil's toy.
Our boat is pulling back, an officer
And several German sailors in her stern.
Now they come up the ladder.
There is a fearless nonchalance, a poise,
A grace about the leader.
He's young, short, dark-haired, dressed in navy blue.
I like him irresistibly.
Our captain greets him, takes him up to his cabin.
Then comes a call, "Can anyone here speak German?"
I'm up the stairway in a flash.
I sense this man will give us a square deal.
He scans our papers and the passenger list,
Reads us a lecture on our ignorance
For not interpreting his flashes,
Tells us next time we see a submarine
To stop at once and send across our papers.
But all the time he's courteous as a guest.
"May I sit down here?"
Then he inspects our cargo,
Declines the offer of a case of whiskey.
"Our captain would enjoy it."
He lines the passengers up
And gets me to repeat a short address:
"Gentlemen and ladies,
I'm sorry to have detained you,
But it is war."
(He says this very simply.)

"We haven't wished for war with England,
 But it was forced on us.
 What should you do
 If somebody came and took your southern coast?
 You wouldn't like it."
 He bows, shakes hands with me.
"We're not so barbarous, are we,
 Though I'm not shaved?" He strokes a silky stubble.
"Well, see you at a tea dance, New York."
 Our lifeboat takes him back. We blow three blasts.
 The sub responds in mellow baritone.
 We wave and cheer; her men cheer back.
 We steam ahead.

"That was the fellow got the *Athenia,*"
 Remarks our little, thin-lipped Maine first officer,
 A gray old sea dog.
 That doesn't make me feel so very good.
 But that was just his guess,
 And when one meets a perfect gentleman,
 What can one do
 But treat him as exactly what he is,
 Even if he comes to one from a submarine?

Since then the trip has been like other trips,
 Till in due time we make and drop Cape Race.
 It's rather comforting to know the earth
 Has still another hemisphere.
 They tell me we have passed Nantucket Lightship.
 D.V., tomorrow we shall reach New York.

Winslow Homer

Rocks against foaming water, black on gray;
    And men, firm-based on schooner deck or dory,
    Themselves like rocks against the gloom and glory
Of mid-sea surges on the Banks. No gay
Bravado of Parisian color-play
    Dilutes the eternal with the transitory.
    Each form a hero's, every scene a story,
Here truth speaks, not the fashion of a day.

Winslow, you bid the billows rear and rush,
    You send the hollow ships to seek their goal,
      And surely stern gray courage from of yore
Is on your palette when you dip the brush,
    For in your mastery we divine the soul
      Of the first Homer by the surf-loud shore.

To Paul Dougherty

On Looking at One of His Paintings

You show us clashing waves and towering shore,
The coast of Cornwall, rugged, purple-gray,
Where gust-blown gulls festoon Tintagel Bay,
And over ridden reefs the billows pour
Their flashing fleece. We guess the broken roar
Comes faint to those who stand or idly stray
On the sheer cliff edge. Daisied nooks of gay
Green turf, that well might tempt a child to play,
Fringe crags where once a castle frowned of yore.

How glorious and how unforgettable
The scene you give us, Paul! It hangs outspread
Before me. Seldom now I hear your name,
Despite past honors, yet there's this to tell.
When Winslow Homer looked at it, he said,
"There's my successor." How ask more of Fame?

Sea Painting by Albert Ryder

A Villanelle

Tumult of cloud, the tossing sea,
A lonely boat, the lone full moon—
Beauty and terror and mystery.

A somber choral chanted in three;
Hull silhouetted (the heart of the tune),
Tumult of cloud, the tossing sea.

Shattering waves glint eerily,
Swift slides the sail through the night's weird noon,
Beauty and terror and mystery.

And the motionless helmsman, what thinks he,
The soul in the trance of this cradling swoon,
Tumult of cloud, the tossing sea?

Thought is lulled in the rhapsody
That thrums his shrouds with a strange wild croon,
Beauty and terror and mystery.

Death? What is death but a life to be,
A vaguer voyage, a dimmer boon:
Tumult of cloud, the tossing sea,
Beauty and terror and mystery.

To The Sea

Whatever your color,
Whatever your form,
Blazing in sunlight,
Dismal in storm,
Silken and purple in Rio's bay,
Green that shatters the crystal spray
On a Cornish headland, or pallid gray
Along Baltic sands—I am yours, O sea,
For the power and beauty you bring to me.

When I am troubled,
My cares find rest,
Cupped by the rim
Of your mighty nest.
When I am weary and spent and dull,
I can skim away like a dipping gull;
And my eyes are glad and my heart is full,
As my soul breaks out in a yearning sweep
From my prisoned self to your boundless deep.

The Joy of Effort

*(For a Bas-Relief of Three Hurdlers
by R. Tait McKenzie)*

Eager as fire, impetuous as the wind,
  They spurn the ground and lightly clear the bar.
Three racers? Nay, three strong wills unconfined,
  Three glad, contending swiftnesses they are;
Three dolphins that with simultaneous leap
  Breast the high breaker of a tropic surge,
As, flashing silvery from the purple deep
  And scattering foam, their curving backs emerge;
Three agile swallows skimming near the ground
  That give their bodies to the buoyant air;
Three roebucks fleet that through the forest bound.
  Yet how can even such with men compare?
Not with mere speed-lust are these forms alive;
The noblest joy of being is to strive.